Original title:
Delphinium Dreams

Copyright © 2025 Creative Arts Management OÜ
All rights reserved.

Author: Charles Whitfield
ISBN HARDBACK: 978-1-80566-728-5
ISBN PAPERBACK: 978-1-80566-857-2

Fables in the Field

In fields where flowers plot and scheme,
The daisies giggle, it seems a dream.
They whisper secrets, oh so sly,
While bumblebees buzz and fly.

Resilient Roots

Roots tangled up in a playful dance,
Raising their leaves, they take a chance.
With every twist, they break the mold,
Telling tales in colors bold.

Garden Chronicles

With carrots gossiping 'neath the dirt,
And lettuce laughing, they wear a skirt.
Tomatoes roll in their vibrant attire,
As peas proclaim they're climbing higher.

In the Shade of Blue

A blue hydrangea, quite a clown,
Wearing a hat that's slightly brown.
It teases bees with its silly show,
Twirling petals in a breezy flow.

Chasing Shadows and Petals

In the garden, shadows play,
Petals giggle while swaying away.
Bumblebees buzz with a jolly tune,
While daisies dance under the spoon.

A squirrel steals a purple crown,
Then slips, tumbling, rolling down.
The flowers chuckle, it's quite the sight,
As he rubs his head and takes to flight.

Ants wear top hats, oh what a show!
They march in lines, putting on a glow.
Confetti made of leaves rains down,
As the garden blooms in a whimsical gown.

With each flutter, the flowers sing,
In a symphony of the silliest fling.
Chasing shadows that twirl and tease,
In a playful world of floral ease.

Secrets of the Flowerbed

In a flowerbed, secrets creep,
Where garden gnomes are fast asleep.
Petite whispers from the buds,
Giggle softly, like sweet floods.

A worm in glasses reads the news,
While sunflowers share their silly views.
The marigolds paint their petals bright,
Claiming they are the stars of the night.

Bees swap stories over a sip,
Of nectar served in a dainty dip.
Tulips giggle as they shake their heads,
At the gossip blooming in flowerbeds.

In this patch, laughter never ends,
Where petals play and all are friends.
Secrets linger in every hue,
A merry world from the morning dew.

A Melody of the Garden

In the garden, melodies rise,
With chirps and buzz and butterfly sighs.
A croquet match for snails all day,
As the flowers cheer with blooms on display.

The tulips trumpet a joyful sound,
Singing songs while spinning around.
Petunias waltz, donning their best,
While dandelions jest and jest.

A robin leads a raucous choir,
As the sun shines with warmth and fire.
Nothing serious in this bright spree,
As nature winks, wild and free.

Frogs play drums on a lily pad stage,
While bees buzz around, releasing rage.
In this melody, laughter stems,
As the garden sings with its leafy gems.

The Language of Blooms

In the whispers of blooms, there's fun to be had,
Where marigolds gossip and roses go mad.
Each petal a story, each leaf a jest,
In a world where humor's always the best.

The orchids claim to hold the crown,
While violets frown and wear a frown.
Petals chuckle under a bright sun,
In a floral joke, they all are one.

Sunflowers giggle with their tall heads,
Over daisies' tales of foolish threads.
Every bud holds a smirk or a grin,
As the colors laugh and spin within.

In the garden's heart, joy blooms wide,
With friends all around, laughter won't hide.
The language of flowers, it must be clear,
Is one of delight, where all foes disappear.

Embracing the Spirit of Blossoms

In the garden, blooms sway tall,
With bees that dance, and butterflies crawl.
Laughter spills from petals bright,
As squirrels perform in daylight's light.

A flower's hat goes for a spin,
A pollen party where bees fit in.
The breeze sends whispers through the leaves,
A ticklish tickle that never deceives.

Echoes in the Quiet Meadow

In the meadow, laughter echoes loud,
As daisies giggle, they gather a crowd.
A rabbit hops, with mischief in eyes,
Chasing butterflies, oh what a surprise!

The grass hums tunes of a silly song,
While tiny ants march, all day long.
They wiggle and squirm, in neat little lines,
Making a joke about their own designs.

Whispers in Blue

Blue blooms blush as the wind does tease,
Wink at the clouds while swaying with ease.
A chatty robin shares a quick joke,
While daisies blush with a playful croak.

They giggle at raindrops, plopping and plink,
Each droplet's bounce makes them rethink.
A snail in a shell thinks he's so grand,
But trips on a petal, oh isn't it bland!

A Tapestry of Petals

Petals weave tales as they flutter and spin,
Creating laughter with each little grin.
The sun peeks in, a cheeky surprise,
Highlighting the mischief in all of their eyes.

A colorful mix, the blooms dance together,
They share all their secrets in sunny weather.
With petals that twinkle like stars after dusk,
Each chuckle they share is a shade of sweet musk.

Beneath the Indigo Sky

Beneath the blue, the daisies dance,
With bees that waltz, they take a chance.
The tulips gossip, oh what a scene,
While snails debate who's fastest in green.

The clouds roll by, in cotton candy,
A squirrel prances, oh so dandy.
The grass is tickling our toes and knees,
As laughter floats on the gentle breeze.

The Garden's Serenade

In the garden, weeds wear crowns of gold,
While carrots tell jokes, a sight to behold.
Charming roses play hide and seek,
And marigolds giggle, oh so unique.

The moonlight twinkles on petals bright,
As crickets sing songs throughout the night.
Sunflowers nod with a comical flair,
In this quirky realm, joy's everywhere!

Dreaming in Lavender Hues

Lavender whispers, secrets galore,
As rabbits hop in with a knock on the door.
The violets cackle, plotting a prank,
While daisies giggle, all perfectly rank.

The wind tells tales, of foolish old gnomes,
Who trip on their hats, far away from their homes.
With each petal's pulse, dreams come alive,
In blooms' happy world, the magic will thrive.

Waltz of the Blooms

The flowers twirl in a vibrant ballet,
While the butterflies lead in their own frolic play.
A daisy lifts her skirt, a perfumed display,
While bees are the drummers, buzzing away.

With lavender spritz, the air is so sweet,
Even grumpy old weeds tap their feet.
In this garden of giggles, the joy just resumes,
As all take a turn in the waltz of the blooms.

Lullabies in Lilac

In the garden where giggles bloom,
Bumblebees wear tiny costumes.
Giggling daisies sway and tease,
Whispering to the lilac breeze.

Squirrels juggle acorns with flair,
While the wind sings without a care.
Butterflies don their caped attire,
Dancing high above the choir.

Frogs in hats croak out their tunes,
Under the gaze of silly moons.
Each petal bursts with laughter's hue,
As the garden smiles at me and you.

Beneath the Blossoms' Gaze

Under trees with bowing limbs,
Bumblebees excel at whims.
Flowers trade their fragrant jokes,
While ants parade in tiny cloaks.

The sun winks, it's time to play,
As petals chuckle through the day.
A ladybug spins like a top,
As butterflies flap and never stop.

Grasshoppers dance with giddy flair,
Twirling round in springtime air.
And daisies whisper, 'Join the fun!'
In this land where pranks are spun.

The Color of Serenity

In fields where laughter paints the sky,
Tulips giggle and daffodils sigh.
Pansies pull pranks with their bright hue,
As the daisies giggle, 'What's new?'

Silly sunflowers chase after bees,
While chubby caterpillars munch on leaves.
The breeze chuckles, bringing light,
To petals that wiggle with delight.

Among the blooms, a jester's ball,
Where colors mingle and laughter calls.
In this wonderland of cheer,
Every moment brings joy near.

Myriad Shades of Tranquility

In a world of colors bright and bold,
Petals gossip secrets untold.
Cacti wear hats made of dreams,
While slumbering squirrels plot their schemes.

A rainbow's laugh spills on the ground,
As flowers converse, all around.
Tickling breeze, a playful tease,
What mischief blooms beneath the trees?

Galloping clouds join in the fun,
While grass blades dance beneath the sun.
In hues of mirth, the garden sings,
Of joy that only nature brings.

Shades of Ecstasy

In a garden where giggles bloom,
The colors swirl, dispelling gloom.
A blue butterfly, full of sass,
Doing the cha-cha, shaking grass.

The bees wear glasses, looking very cool,
While ants line dance, breaking every rule.
A dog in shades, lounging in the sun,
Claims he's the king; oh, what fun!

The Enchantment of Faded Petals

Petals fall like whispers soft,
A clumsy breeze sends them aloft.
They tumble down, pirouette wide,
Making giggly ghosts that glide.

With each bright hue, they joke and tease,
As clouds roll in, they dance with ease.
A flower's hat, too big, too bright,
Says, 'I'm the star tonight, alright!'

Brushed by the Whispering Breeze

A breeze tickles the merry leaves,
With jokes so silly, it never leaves.
It whispers tales of cats in hats,
And dogs who think they're acrobats.

The grass giggles as bugs perform,
A jitterbug dance, no need for norm.
With each rustle, laughter grows,
As tumbleweeds put on their shows.

In the Embrace of Serenity

Calmness wraps the world so tight,
Yet ants in tuxedos cause delight.
While daisies gossip, smiles abound,
A breeze sneezes, all tumble around.

The sun hums tunes of silly cheer,
As butterflies laugh, oh so near.
In this jest of flora's grace,
Every petal wears a smiling face.

Hues of Forgotten Enchantment

In a garden where colors squawk,
The petals gossip as they talk.
A bee in a bowtie, oh what a sight,
Stumbles through blooms, it's quite a flight.

The daisies giggle, the roses yell,
A squirrel shares secrets, oh, what the hell!
Chasing a butterfly, forgot the route,
Leaves are laughing, that's their hoot.

Sunflowers wear shades, looking so fly,
Cacti dance wildly, reaching for the sky.
The vines are entwined in a silly embrace,
A funny parade in this leafy place.

So come take a stroll past the tulip lanes,
Where laughter blooms and joy remains.
In hues forgotten, where silliness blooms,
Magic is real in these floral rooms.

Dancing with the Windflowers

At dawn, they twirl, these quirky blooms,
Swaying in rhythm, no room for glooms.
With petals like skirts, they flaunt in the breeze,
Tickled by whispers of playful tease.

A dandelion queen with a tell-tale crown,
Holds court with the daisies, never a frown.
They giggle and wiggle, what a funny crew,
Offering sunflower hats, if you only knew.

The tulips trip over each other with glee,
Doing a jig as if setting them free.
With pollen for confetti, they shower the air,
Spreading pure joy everywhere, unaware.

In this floral fiesta, the windflowers sway,
Turning the garden into a cabaret.
A gathering of petals, pure delights,
Dancing with laughter, under the lights.

Serenade in Indigo

Deep in the garden where shadows play,
Indigo petals lead the way.
A chorus of flowers sings out loud,
Arm in arm with the giggly crowd.

Moonlight sprinkles a silver hue,
While lilacs whisper secrets, just a few.
A frog with a top hat croaks out a tune,
Enticing the crickets beneath the moon.

The lilies prance like they own the night,
With roots all tangled, they hold on tight.
Bumblebees buzz like they took the stage,
As wilting vines put on a funny rage.

In this serenade, nothing's absurd,
As petals chuckle in every word.
An indigo night, full of laughter's charm,
A whimsical garden, where no one comes to harm.

Secrets of the Garden Night

Under the stars where the shadows creep,
The plants are plotting while the world's asleep.
With whispers of petals, they share their dreams,
And giggle at the moon's buttery beams.

The nightingale practices silly songs,
While daffodils dance among the throngs.
Of worms in tuxedos, oh what a night,
Carousel dreams in the soft moonlight.

A hedgehog in glasses, reading a tome,
Wonders if flowers should learn to roam.
The roses roll over, sharing their plight,
Confessing the secrets of garden night.

With twinkling laughter and stories unfurled,
This botanic realm spins a whimsical world.
Giving life to whispers, in a patch of delight,
In secrets they share, everything feels right.

Floral Enigmas

In the garden, blooms take flight,
Wobbling petals, such a sight!
Bees wear tiny sunglasses now,
While squirrels dance, I take a bow.

Tulips argue with the vines,
Over whose shade is more divine.
Roses gossip, oh so sweet,
While daisies tap their tiny feet.

Sunflowers turn their heads to chat,
With daisies dressed in polka-dot!
Laughter rings, as colors clash,
In this world, dreams make a splash.

Petunias don a hat so wide,
As they giggle, full of pride.
The garden's buzzing with delight,
As flowers party through the night.

The Essence of Growth

Once a seed, now quite the sprout,
Laughing loudly, there's no doubt.
Stretching limbs to touch the sky,
Chasing bugs, oh my, oh my!

The carrots giggle underground,
With radishes, a silly sound.
A garden crew, so full of cheer,
Inventing games, year after year.

Tomatoes blush in sunny glow,
While zucchini puts on quite a show.
They roll and tumble, what a sight,
Nature's antics, pure delight!

In this patch, the laughter flows,
With new beginnings, anything goes.
Watch us grow, with hearts so light,
Turning chores to pure delight.

Dreams in the Den

In a cozy den, where wild things play,
There's giggles, grins, and bright bouquet.
Mice wear shoes, and cats wear hats,
Conversations held with friendly bats.

Bunnies bounce to a jazzy beat,
While hedgehogs tap their tiny feet.
With chatter swirling like the breeze,
The flowers weave through giggling trees.

Pillows soft, a fluffy floor,
Pastel petals, dreams galore.
A whimsical world of fun and cheer,
Laughing and dancing, all sincere.

Join the fun, let the laughter rise,
In this garden under moonlit skies.
With every bloom, a secret shared,
In our den, dreams are declared!

A Palette of Whispers

Colors chat in hushed delight,
Chasing rainbows, day and night.
Yellow giggles, blue replies,
As green winks with sparkly eyes.

Each hue has its own funny tale,
Of windy trips and daydream trails.
Violets tease the fuchsia pink,
While oranges twirl and dance, they think.

Splatters of laughter fill the air,
As colors clash without a care.
With every brushstroke, joy unfolds,
In this canvas, laughter molds.

So let the colors dance and sway,
Creating stories in a playful way.
With every shade a joke to share,
In this palette, life's a flair!

Between Petal and Star

In a garden where gnomes play,
The flowers gossip in a silly way.
A bee stumbles over its own flight,
Chasing a bloom in a comical plight.

With petals so blue, they tickle the sky,
A ladybug winks as she zooms by.
The sun sneezes brightly, a glittering burst,
And clouds giggle softly, quenching their thirst.

Squirrels debate who's the fairest of all,
While butterflies dance, having a ball.
In this patch of color where laughter rings clear,
Every blossom whispers, "Come join the cheer!"

So pick up a flower, give it a twirl,
Join in the fun of this petaled swirl.
For laughter and joy make the best kind of art,
In the magic found between petal and star.

Cascade of Celestial Colors

A splash of colors, what a sight!
Rabbits in bow ties hop with delight.
The daisies giggle, they can't keep still,
While painting the town with a whimsical thrill.

From purple to pink, the hues collide,
A rainbow of puns takes you for a ride.
Each lily's a comedian, funny and spry,
While tulips crack jokes about clouds in the sky.

A butterfly slips on dew-dappled grass,
As the daisies chime in, "Oh, what a pass!"
The sun does a jig, a twinkling spree,
In the cascade of color, wild and free.

So come join the revel, dance under the sun,
In a garden where laughter has just begun.
Where every petal dances, a sight full of glee,
In a world painted bright with pure jubilee.

The Language of Blossoms

In the language of blooms, there's humor to find,
With every tickle of wind, they jest and unwind.
The violets gossip, with petals so grand,
While squirrels play charades in this laughter-filled land.

Roses debate if they're truly that red,
As daisies propose, "Let's amuse our friends instead!"
A tulip trips lightly, takes a misstep,
And all of the lilies join in for a pep.

Bumblebees laugh as they buzz on their quest,
Searching for nectar, they're quite the jest.
With petals that chatter and colors that gleam,
This garden of laughter feels like a dream.

So, listen closely, to the jokes they unfold,
In the language of blossoms, pure joy to behold.
A riot of chuckles beneath the bright sun,
Where every bloom whispers, "Life's just begun!"

Lullaby for the Wandering Heart

Underneath the starlit skies,
Where flowers hold court with sleepy eyes.
A noontime nap turns into a spree,
As petals sway gently, in harmony.

Forget-me-nots giggle, "Please don't snore,"
While daisies dream of adventures galore.
A sleepy bumblebee hums his refrain,
"Dream of the nectar, and sunny disdain."

Petals sway softly, a lullaby sweet,
Where marshmallow clouds and laughter meet.
The nightingale croons to the flowers below,
In this garden of mirth, where funny hearts grow.

So drift off to slumber, let worries depart,
In this whimsical haven for the wandering heart.
With stars as your blanket and laughter your light,
Dream of the blossoms that dance in the night.

Petal Halos at Dusk

In the garden a cat wears a crown,
Made of petals, pink and brown.
He struts with pride, all puffed and grand,
While flowers giggle, doing a dance band.

The bees become jesters, buzzing in rhyme,
They whisper to flowers, 'We're never on time!'
With pollen-drenched jokes that float in the air,
These moments of silliness without a care.

A butterfly trips, laughs fill the scene,
Falling on daisies in a dress of green.
The sun dips low, the shadows play sweet,
As petals laugh now, with tiny feet.

So join in the fun, in this twilight bright,
Where flowers wear halos and dance in delight.
Forget all the worries, let laughter bloom,
In this patch of joy, there's always room.

Blooming Reflections

Reflections giggle in the pond's cool glance,
As lilies wiggle, making a splashy dance.
The frogs in tuxedos, quite overdressed,
Croak silly ballads, they're truly obsessed.

A sunflower hollers, 'I'm the best in the game!'
While daisies chuckle, remembering their fame.
They trade funny stories of how they could grow,
Each tale a bloom in this wild garden show.

With petals like confetti, they wave in the breeze,
A bouquet of laughter rustling the leaves.
The moon starts to rise, dressed in a wink,
As flowers gather round, ready to think.

In this canvas of chaos, joy's the true key,
With laughter aplenty, we're as happy as can be.
So let's paint the night with giggles anew,
In the garden of dreams where laughter just grew.

The Soft Approach of Twilight

Twilight whispers, secrets so sweet,
As petals gather, for a playful meet.
The stars dress in giggles, twinkling so bright,
While flowers tease shadows, poking with light.

A rose made a joke, 'Hey, ivy, you vine!'
While petunias snickered, 'We're feeling just fine!'
With the breeze as their partner, they giggled with glee,
Embracing the magic of this nursery spree.

Crickets are comedians, chirping their lines,
A theater of nature where humor combines.
The grass rolls its eyes, it's heard all before,
But in this twilight laughter, there's always more.

So let the night settle with chuckles around,
Where petals drift in laughter, all merrily bound.
With each soft approach, let joy be the guide,
In this goofy garden, where laughter resides.

A Dance in Blooming Shades

The flowers host parties in colors so bright,
With poppies in polka dots, a wonderful sight.
The tulips play tag with their long, graceful necks,
While orchids do twirls, in sequined specks.

A daffodil diva sings high on a stem,
While daisies join in, a cheerful anthem.
The clovers do cartwheels, and all start to cheer,
A dance floor of petals, oh what a sphere!

With laughter like bubbles, they float in the haze,
As the sun dips below, they twirl in a maze.
The wind plays a tune, a whimsical beat,
As flowers join in, with their jolly feet.

So frolic with friends, let the night be our stage,
Where blooms dance in laughter, as joy turns the page.
In this garden of giggles and bright little gales,
Find fun in the petals, where laughter prevails.

Garden of Endless Hopes

In the garden where wishes bloom,
The gnomes juggle on pots with a boom.
I whispered to weeds, 'Don't be alarmed!'
They giggled and swayed, utterly charmed.

Butterflies wearing polka-dot ties,
Play hopscotch beneath the sunny skies.
The daisies in dresses tango and twirl,
While snails in a race give it a whirl!

A squirrel in shades winks at the sun,
With acorns as prizes, he's ready for fun.
The roses all dance on their petals so bright,
And moonbeams come out just to join in the light.

In this garden of giggles and glee,
Every flower blooms happily free.
With laughter as water, our dreams take flight,
In this wild, wacky, and whimsical site.

Dances with the Wind

A dandelion fluffs a regal crown,
As the breeze ties ribbons, swirling around.
Grasshoppers start an impromptu show,
While clouds take bets on who'll steal the glow.

Hats off to the daisies, all in a row,
They nod and they dance, putting on a show.
Ants march in formation, a troops' parade,
While a butterfly's wings make a grand escapade.

The sun plays peek-a-boo, giggling bright,
As tulips in bowties dance through the night.
The wind knows the steps, oh so divine,
And laughter is found with each twist of vine.

What a night for a jolly jubilee,
With whispers and chuckles disguised in the breeze.
Join the petals in their playful delight,
In the dance of the wind, everything feels right.

Blooming Thoughts

In a patch of petals, ideas collide,
Where bees write poems, they take care to hide.
The sunflowers grin, with heads held so high,
While ladybugs gasp at the butterfly fly-by.

The lilacs tickle, just for a laugh,
As squirrels debate the funniest gaffe.
Roses spill secrets over cups of tea,
While the ferns sigh and laugh in glee.

A parade of thoughts springs forward to play,
With every bright bud sharing its way.
It's a carnival stage for each silly whim,
As blooms make a mockery on a floral hymn.

There's no sadness here, only joy on display,
In the garden where chuckles and giggles hold sway.
As blooms share their jokes, with laughter alight,
In this riot of colors, everything feels right.

Imagery of the Twilight Garden

In a twilight garden, with shadows that creep,
The flowers tell stories while frogs sing their leap.
Moonflowers giggle, tipping their hats,
As crickets recite all their best acrobats.

Fireflies blink as they board the train,
To ride through the dusk, chasing silly fame.
The roses gossip about sweet midnight snacks,
While ivy plants weave fantastical hacks.

The pathway glimmers with mischievous light,
As echoes of laughter pierce through the night.
A poppy in pajamas adopts a sly grin,
Claiming it's party time, let the fun begin!

With whimsy and wonder in every last part,
This garden of dreams grips the whimsical heart.
As the moon rises high and the laughter takes flight,
In the twilight embrace, everything feels right.

Floral Reflections

In gardens full of laughter, blooms grow wide,
The flowers gossip softly, side by side.
A daisy winks, a tulip gives a shout,
They trade their secrets, with petals flung about.

Bees wear tiny glasses, buzzing through the air,
While butterflies wear bows, with plenty style to spare.
The roses roll their eyes at every witty jest,
As violets giggle, never one to rest.

Sunshine spills like lemonade, so sweet and bright,
Pansies play charades until the fall of night.
A sunflower wearing shades is quite the sight,
Under a blue sky, everything feels right.

With each bloom's laughter, the garden beams,
Nature's a jester, bursting at the seams.
In each petal's dance, joy takes center stage,
As the floral antics write poetry on the page.

The Dance of Starlit Blooms

Underneath the moonlight, blossoms take the floor,
Forget-me-nots are twirling, wanting more and more.
Petunias in a line, do the conga with flair,
While daisies shake their stems, without a care.

Laughter echoes softly, as nightingales sing,
Each bloom is a dancer, a colorful fling.
The shadows hum a tune, bright as a spark,
As blooms in polka dots light up the dark.

Tulips trip and tumble, giggling with delight,
In this floral disco, everything feels right.
They spin in circles, underneath the stars,
While dandelions float by, giggling at the cars.

Joy radiates through petals, as they laugh and sway,
Nature's very own party, come join the play!
In every stem's embrace, fun fills the space,
Where blossoms paint the night with cheerful grace.

Beneath the Canciones of Nature

A lilac hums a tune in soft, sweet song,
While marigolds chime in, singing all day long.
With grasshoppers drumming, the symphony begins,
As flowers sway together, with playful grins.

In the breeze, the petals gossip light and free,
They trade old tales of bees with glee.
The clovers crack a joke, a pun that's quite bold,
As peonies giggle, their laughter uncontrolled.

Above them, clouds chuckle, watching blooms below,
While thorns play hide and seek, putting on a show.
With every breeze that passes, joy gets a boost,
As flowers share their laughter, in nature's wild roost.

Together they create a concert of delight,
Underneath the sun and stars, all day and night.
In these floral songs, humor takes its flight,
A tapestry of giggles, in vibrant hues so bright.

Symphony of Color and Light

In a garden where laughter reigns over the earth,
Each petal brings a smile, and a joyful mirth.
Dancing colors mingle, a jolly parade,
As sunflowers whistle tunes, in the light they wade.

Every snapdragon ready, with a cheeky sway,
While buttercups challenge, who can laugh the most today?
The tulips tease the lilies, with banter so sweet,
In this floral orchestra, their joy can't be beat.

With every shade they wear, humor blooms anew,
The daisies throw a party, with a dash of dew.
Every bud has stories, laughter in each line,
As the wind carries notes of their playful design.

Under a bright sky, they twirl and sing,
Each flower a note in this joyful spring.
In this symphony of colors, laughter takes flight,
Nature's own orchestra, a vibrant delight.

Radiance Within the Thicket

In a forest of giggles, the flowers do sway,
A squirrel wearing shoes has come out to play.
With a dance and a twirl, he jumps on a log,
Chasing shadows and dreams like a bright little frog.

The sun tickles leaves, and the branches all wiggle,
While a gnome on a toad sings a tune with a giggle.
Toadstools in laughter, they're having a feast,
With the jests of the woods, they've invited a beast.

Under twinkling stars, the moon takes a peek,
To join in the chorus of a night that's unique.
A rabbit in glasses reads poems on bark,
While the fireflies twinkle and light up the dark.

So come join the merriment, the laughter and cheer,
Though the thicket may seem a bit quirky and queer.
With each step you take, let your joy intertwine,
In the radiance of fun, where the moonbeams all shine.

Butterflies and Breaths

A butterfly winks with a wink so absurd,
As it dangles upside-down, like a clumsy bird.
It flutters toward flowers, some nose to the ground,
Tickling petals with giggles and joys all around.

With a sigh and a flutter, they take to the sky,
And dance with the wind, oh my, oh my!
But a daisy takes flight, and it twirls in surprise,
While a party of bees buzz in marvelous pies.

In the laughter of petals, where light starts to spin,
A caterpillar chuckles, "Am I shy or just thin?"
As the blooms burst with colors, each hue makes a jest,
In this whimsical garden, we'll all feel our best.

So breathe in the joy, let it color your day,
For in this ballet, no two moves are gray.
With every small giggle, the air fills with cheer,
And butterflies dance with a flair, oh dear!

Summer's Soft Cloak

Beneath summer's blanket, the sun does a jig,
While grasshoppers boast, each little green pig.
A picnic is brewing with snacks piled high,
But the ants have a plan, as they march on by.

With lemonade rivers and sandwiches tall,
There's pickleball chaos, the best game of all.
The sun smiles down on this whimsical spree,
As the ketchup steals mustard—oh what a decree!

A hammock of dreams swings in lazy revere,
While squirrels tell tall tales of the berries they steer.
With blossoms a-giggle and clouds dressed in glee,
Each moment is blushing, what fun it would be!

So don summer's cloak and enjoy the delight,
For laughter's the key to make everything bright.
With a wink and a smile, let your worries float by,
And join in the magic beneath the blue sky.

Luminescent Nights

When the moon wears a cape and the stars start to wink,
The fireflies gather for a night filled with ink.
They scribble their tales on the breeze like a story,
While crickets compose tunes of midnight's great glory.

A raccoon in spectacles peruses the show,
With popcorn in paws, as he chuckles below.
In the shimmer of darkness, they gather with flair,
For the dance of the nighttime is beyond compare.

The owls in their wisdom hoot jokes to the sky,
While glowworms are working their glow-in-the-eye.
Each giggle resounds with the softest delight,
As the moon beams down on this whimsical night.

So tiptoe through wonders where laughter ignites,
With a dash of silliness, the heart takes its flights.
In the magical shimmer, where dreams take their spin,
Let the glow of the night bring out the joy within.

The Art of Blooming

In gardens where the petals twirl,
A flower thinks it's quite the girl.
It fluffs its crown, and strikes a pose,
While bees parade in fancy clothes.

The sunlight's kiss, a golden tease,
Each blossom giggles in the breeze.
With each small sway, they laugh and play,
Deciding who'll steal the show today.

Roses pout and daisies cheer,
As tulips boast, 'We're here, we're here!'
While pansies grin, a colorful sight,
Proclaiming they're the star of the night.

So if you find a quirky bloom,
Just know it's plotting its own room.
In nature's court, a flower's dream,
Is full of fun, or so it seems.

Enveloping the Breeze

Whispers dance on petals bright,
As flowers flirt with morning light.
The daisies wink, the lilies laugh,
While roses pose for the yearbook staff.

With every gust, a giggle flows,
Blowing kisses, do you suppose?
The violets smirk, 'We're the best!'
While poppies snore, taking a rest.

In sunlit fields, they form a band,
With nature's rhythm, they take a stand.
Each leaf a member, each stem a pose,
Blooming boldly, striking a rose.

When day turns dark and stars come out,
They share their tales with joyous shout.
In every breeze, a story spins,
Of floral antics and leafy wins.

A Reverie in Fuchsia

In fields of fuchsia, laughter plays,
With petals dancing through the days.
The flowers chat of cheeky schemes,
While butterflies burst forth in dreams.

They giggle low, whisper up high,
Debating who just touched the sky.
The bees roll by, all buzz and cheer,
'Our nectar's sweet, let's all come near!'

With every bloom, a story grows,
Of sunny days and friendly foes.
The sun dips low, it's time for fun,
As flowers sparkle, one by one.

And when the night unveils its grace,
Each blossom finds its cozy place.
Under the moon, they share a grin,
In dreams of pink, the laughter spins.

The Kaleidoscope of Flora

In gardens filled with colors bright,
Each flower strives for morning's light.
With twisty stems and frilly gowns,
They compete for smiles, not frowns.

Lilies leap like they're in a race,
While petunias blush in their grace.
A marigold claims it's the best,
As sunflowers tower, full of zest.

'Look at me!' says every bloom,
'I'll chase away your gloomiest gloom.'
With every bounce, a chuckle's heard,
The petals giggle, not a word.

As twilight falls, they close their eyes,
Yet in their hearts, the laughter lies.
For flowers know that life's a game,
In blooming joy, they stake their claim.

Whispers of Blue Petals

In a garden where giggles grow,
Petals tickle toes, don't you know?
Bees wear tiny hats all day,
Buzzing jokes, come out to play!

Wind whispers secrets, oh so sly,
Tickling flowers as they sigh.
Sunshine grins with a wink so bright,
Chasing shadows, what a delight!

Butterflies dance in silly shoes,
Flapping colors, bright and profuse.
Each bloom erupts in fits of glee,
Nature's laughter, wild and free!

Watch the daisies do the twist,
Swaying gently, can't resist.
Petals gossip, oh what a scene,
In the garden, a laugh routine!

Echoes of a Summer Sky

Up above, the clouds wear hats,
Frolicking like silly cats.
Sunbeams throw a party wide,
Join the fun, come inside!

A dandelion blows a kiss,
A wishful sigh, a cheeky bliss.
Stars in daydreams, bright and bold,
Spinning tales, laughter untold!

Kites are dancing, caught in flight,
Telling secrets, oh what a sight!
Rainbow ribbons weave the air,
Making mischief everywhere!

Clouds tumble like playful clowns,
Dancing high above the towns.
The breeze sings a funny tune,
Underneath the jolly moon!

Beneath the Azure Veil

Beneath the blue, where giggles bloom,
Ladybugs dance, creating room.
With every flutter, a joke is told,
Whisking smiles, breaking the mold!

Squirrels wear glasses, reading maps,
Plotting antics, all sorts of jabs.
The groundhogs cheer with furry applause,
As flowers laugh without a pause!

Sprinkles of sunlight tickle the ground,
Where silly critters can be found.
Each laugh echoes through the trees,
Join the revelry, if you please!

The petals caper, giving chase,
In this wacky, vibrant space.
Nature's stage, so rich and grand,
With every bloom, a mishap planned!

Twilight Blooming

As twilight whispers, stars appear,
Flowers giggle, full of cheer.
Crickets chirp, creating tunes,
Underneath the laughing moons!

The roses tease with velvety flair,
Budding jokes with fragrant air.
In the patch, the tulips stand,
Telling tales, hand in hand!

Marigolds twirl in bright attire,
Seeking the spotlight, never tire.
The night blooms with laughter galore,
Whimsical wonders forever more!

Petals shimmer in twilight's embrace,
Breaking into a silly race.
In this garden, where laughter springs,
Every flower is a queen with wings!

Reveries in Violet

In the garden, blooms dance bold,
Petals giggle, stories unfold.
Bees wear hats, buzzing with glee,
Tickling the flowers, oh what a spree!

Butterflies sip from cups of dew,
In their frocks of purple, they twirl and woo.
A snail in shades of violet glares,
While the daisies gossip in flirty pairs.

Worms in bowties dig with flair,
While playful fairies toss in the air.
A clever toad with a jolly shout,
Sings of secrets as he leaps about.

So in this realm, where laughter fleeting,
The flowers smile, their perfume greeting.
In lilac laughter, joy is found,
With each silly dance, we twirl around.

Whimsy Amongst the Stalks

Among the stalks of vibrant hue,
A radish braces for a view.
It dreams of dancing, what a sight!
But trips on greens and flops in delight.

Carrots wear shades, looking so cool,
While peas debate who's top of the school.
A lone tomato rushes and slips,
Giggling loudly as he catches his flips.

In this patchwork of quirky sights,
A sunflower captured by moonlit nights.
Spinning tales of a veggie crew,
With punchlines that start anew!

Here, every leaf has laughter stored,
In a secret garden of joy adored.
So come join the fun, don't be shy,
Wrap yourself in whimsy and let laughter fly!

Echoing Blooms

Petals whisper, secrets shared,
In wind's soft laugh, nothing's spared.
A jester bee with stripes so bright,
Buzzes his tune, an echoing light.

Chasing shadows, blooms play hide,
In their colorful coats, they take pride.
A cat in sunbeams chases a fly,
Hits a tulip, oh my, oh my!

The daisies chuckle, the lilacs squirm,
As a wise old crow starts to affirm.
"Laugh while you bloom, tomorrow is hush,
So spread your joy in a purple rush!"

In this garden, the echoes ring,
With jokes sprouting on every wing.
Time winks at us, chuckling low,
As petals dance in delightful show.

Petal by Petal

Petal by petal, laughter grows,
In sunlight's kiss, the funny flows.
A daffodil slips, then does a spin,
While a silly bug wears a tiny grin.

A laughing bud, fresh with delight,
Bouncing on stems, full of bright light.
"Hold my pollen!" the clovers shout,
As they jumble in a jovial rout.

Tulips tickle with a cheeky tease,
While sweet peas sway, adrift in the breeze.
A bumblebee crashes, awkwardly bold,
And flowers erupt in laughter untold.

So we join in, in this frolicsome sprawl,
As petals reveal their mirthful call.
In this garden, where smiles are set,
Petal by petal, we won't forget!

Vignettes in Violets

In a field so wild and grand,
A flower took a stand.
It wore a hat with style so bright,
The bees came buzzing, what a sight!

The daisies giggled, oh so loud,
To see a flower so very proud.
It danced in breezes, swayed with glee,
Declaring, 'Look, I'm fancy free!'

With petals spread, it stole the show,
And made the sunflowers feel low.
The tulips rolled their eyes in jest,
While clovers said, 'We wish you best!'

But then a wind, oh what a tease,
Tipped over that hat with greatest ease.
The flower blushed, a sheepish grin,
'I'll just wear leaves, let the fun begin!'

So under skies, both blue and bright,
The flower danced with all its might.
In laughter shared, we found our way,
In fields of jest, where blooms would play.

Nature's Gentle Embrace

In the woods where laughter treads,
A squirrel slipped on flower beds.
With acorns bouncing, oh what fun,
He danced beneath the warming sun!

The songbirds chirped a silly tune,
As butterflies began to swoon.
A ladybug with polka dots,
Declared herself the queen of pots.

But then the breeze, a naughty prank,
Gave three bugs a splashing tank.
In puddles deep, with wiggly feet,
They hosted a dance, quite the feat!

The flowers clapped, their petals wide,
As nature's ball took joyful stride.
With laughter ringing through the trees,
The world was wrapped in silly ease.

Beneath the branches, peace would team,
In nature's grasp, a vibrant dream.
With every chuckle shared aloud,
Together, we formed a merry crowd!

The Heart of the Meadow

In a meadow bright with colors bold,
A flower whispered tales untold.
It claimed to hold the sun's warm rays,
And juggled pollen in playful ways.

The bumblebees rolled, with quite a buzz,
They tiptoed past, causing a fuss.
'We are the kings of bloom today!'
Cried one bee, in a dapper way.

But then a breeze, it gave a shove,
And toppled blooms with gentle love.
'Oh no, my flair!' the petals sighed,
As daisies laughed, and violets pried.

Yet through the tumble, joy arose,
With laughter shared among the rows.
The heart of the meadow beat with cheer,
In every giggle, nature near.

So let us twirl in this floral spree,
Where every flower finds its key.
An ode to life, in colors bright,
In the heart of the meadow, pure delight!

Flourish and Flight

In the garden where giggles grow,
A butterfly put on a show.
It flitted close, then flew so high,
'Take that, you plants!' it teased with a sigh.

The flowers cheered, their petals wide,
As garden gnomes danced side by side.
'We'll flourish here, on roots so fine,
While butterflies sip on nectar wine!'

But then a cat stretched, oh so sly,
It waved its tail with a lazy sigh.
'What's all this fuss?' the kitty proclaimed,
As blooms shimmied, unabashed and unchained.

And so they played a game of chase,
Pollen flying all over the place.
With bursts of laughter, joy ignites,
In a world of flourish and flights.

So here we dance, in colors bright,
Where laughter swells, pure delight.
With every turn, we find our sound,
In gardens where happiness is found!

Meditations in the Meadow

In a field where daisies sway,
Thoughts of cupcakes drift away.
Bouncing bees with tiny flaps,
Plotting schemes for nectar laps.

Worms in ties, they squirm and dance,
Planning their next wiggly prance.
Grasshoppers giggle, frogs just croak,
Who knew plants could tell a joke?

Sunshine tickles every leaf,
Silly squirrels play hide and thief.
Clouds above draw funny shapes,
A rabbit dreams of superhero capes.

In this haven jokes abound,
Nature's laughter all around.
A picnic spread with fruit to share,
Was that a sandwich? No, a bear!

The Pathway of Starlit Flowers

Under twinkling lanterns bright,
Flowers gossip through the night.
Petals whisper silly rhymes,
Swapping secrets, trading limes.

Moonlight casts a goofy gaze,
Butterflies in sparkling haze.
Dancing shadows take a twirl,
Spinning like a dizzy whirl.

Crickets chirp a playful song,
As fireflies hum along.
A tulip winks, a rose will pout,
In a floral shout-out bout.

Sprinklers sprinkle, giggles rise,
A garden full of sweet surprise.
Nature's pranks are on full show,
Who knew flowers had this flow?

A Journey of Color

Colors burst in laugh and cheer,
Painting paths that waver near.
With laughter blooming all around,
Each blossom wears a joyous crown.

A violet wears a polka dot,
While roses sport a wild plot.
Sunflowers turn their heads in mirth,
Who knew they held such chuckle's worth?

Buttercups play peek-a-boo,
While daisies sing a jolly tune.
Tulips with their heads held high,
Join the revelry, oh my!

Every hue a vibrant jest,
Nature's palette at its best.
A playful stroll, a laugh-filled prize,
In this canvas, joy will rise!

Brushstrokes of Nature

With colors splashed on leafy bounds,
Nature's humor knows no grounds.
A painter's brush, a wiggly line,
Creating laughter, oh how divine!

Roses giggle with a sneeze,
While daisies dance in the breeze.
A canvas stretched with joyful hues,
Red and yellow, purple blues.

The wind hums tunes of silly lore,
A sepia squirrel asks for more.
In this gallery, art's alive,
A playful jerk, a jive to strive.

Brushstrokes swirl in merry glee,
Creating moments wild and free.
With every paint dripped from the skies,
Nature's laughter never dies!

Blossoming Horizons

In a garden of giggles, the flowers will sway,
With petals like laughter, they dance in the day.
Bees buzzing jokes that make daisies cheer,
While tulips roll eyes at the sun's bright leer.

The roses wear hats, very silly indeed,
While violets gossip about all the weeds.
A daffodil trips on its own golden frill,
And winks at the wind with a charming thrill.

Butterflies chuckle, they flutter around,
Making fun of the bumblebees' bumbling sounds.
A humorous breeze tickles all in its path,
As flowers all giggle, and nature just laughs.

In this silly garden, with smiles so wide,
Every blossom's a comedian, petals of pride.
So dance with the daisies, let worries take flight,
In a world full of joy, everything feels right.

The Horizon's Floral Song

The sun made a promise to smile every morn,
While daisies all chuckled in colorful scorn.
With stems like a jester, they bow and they sway,
Singing songs to the clouds that float by in play.

Tulips in clusters create quite the show,
With snickers and nudges, they put on a glow.
A marigold whispers, "Why do we wear shoes?"
As pansies burst out in their bright yellow hues.

Phlox on a stage, with a crown made of green,
Cracks jokes to the zinnias, making them keen.
The lilacs all giggle, they can't stop the tease,
As petals erupt with the fun of the breeze.

So stand in the garden, let laughter unfurl,
With flowers all singing in soft, flowery twirl.
With hues so delightful and scents so sublime,
Every blossom a tune, creating sweet rhyme.

Introspection Amongst the Stalks

In a meadow of thoughts, where humor takes flight,
The flowers debate if they're wrong or they're right.
A sunflower proclaims with a big, golden grin,
"Why worry so much? Just let the fun in!"

The lavender laughs with a soft, soothing tone,
While snapdragons tease, "Please don't use a phone!"
A poppy makes faces, all silly and bright,
As petals walk past on their own, filled with fright.

With a wink from the daisies, and giggles from thyme,
The foliage shares secrets in rhythm and rhyme.
In rows they sit pondering, not taking a stance,
As butterflies join in, entranced by the dance.

So here in the stalks, introspection takes bloom,
While flowers all chuckle and banish the gloom.
Their thoughts float like seeds in the cool summer air,
Embracing the funny, releasing all care.

Canvas of Blushing Blossoms

On a canvas of colors, the blossoms take flight,
With petals that giggle, they brighten the night.
A painter with splashes of pink and of blue,
   Chortles at roses, each brushstrokes anew.

The canvas gets tickled as violets collide,
   While lilies burst out in a colorful ride.
With swirls in the air, they mix harmoniously,
   Like a fun little party, a wild jubilee.

Critters parade, painting murals in fun,
While nature joins in, oh, how they will run!
A rabbit humorously hops 'round the scene,
   Chasing after colors, a true artist's dream.

So let's raise a brush to the blossoms that cheer,
For laughter in gardens brings joy ever near.
With strokes of delight, and a splash 'gainst the green,
   This canvas of blooms holds the funniest scene.

Enchanted Stems

In a garden where laughter blooms,
Silly flowers jive and zoom.
Petals wiggle, roots do dance,
Sunlight drips like sweet romance.

With bees in hats and butterflies,
They throw a bash beneath bright skies.
Each bloom dons a comical grin,
As nature's show is set to begin.

The daisies boast of grand tall tales,
While poppies plot their secret trails.
A sunflower dons spectacles wide,
Watching all, from their leafy ride.

But when the moon begins to rise,
These jokers sleep, to dream of pies.
In shadows deep, their whims take flight,
And morning calls them back to light.

Echoes of the Fields

In fields where giggles twist and turn,
The daisies plot, while shadows learn.
Cornflowers burst like laughter bright,
As wind joins in for pure delight.

A clumsy ant trips over dew,
Stumbling past blooms in an awkward queue.
While grasshoppers solo feel so free,
They leap to heights that tickle glee!

Through petals bright, the whispers soar,
Sharing secrets of days of yore.
Sunflowers chuckle, swaying slow,
Endless antics, what a show!

The moon giggles, casting a beam,
As flowers gather in a dream.
Whispers drift through the nightly charms,
Echoes fill fields with laughter's arms.

A Symphony of Sprouts

Sprouts arise with a funky beat,
Each little leaf tapping its feet.
The carrots, decked in bright orange wear,
Join the rhythm without a care.

Zucchinis boast their leafy flair,
While radishes declare they're rare.
They jive and twist, a veggie band,
Making music with a wooden stand.

Tomatoes roll and ketchup flows,
While beans spin tales nobody knows.
The squash declares it's a solo night,
Performing antics to pure delight.

But as the sun succumbs to sleep,
The sprouts grow quiet, their giggles deep.
In dreams they dance, in wild array,
A symphony of sprout-powered play.

When Flowers Sing

When flowers sing, their voices blend,
A chorus bright, it never ends.
Tulips trumpet a joyful sound,
While violets swirl and twirl around.

Roses laugh with petals wide,
Dancing along with ferny pride.
The lilies sway, so graceful and spry,
Creating tunes that float up high.

Dandelions flicker in the breeze,
Their fluffy heads, a jest with ease.
Breezes join with a gentle tease,
Making music that's sure to please.

As night draws near, the songbirds wane,
And flowers hush, till dawn, they strain.
In dreams they hum their playful ring,
Awakening in the joy of spring.

The Promise of Morning Dew

In dawn's soft light, the world awakes,
A turtle slipped, but oh, it fakes!
Its shell a glimmer, bright and round,
It rolls away without a sound.

The raindrops dance on leaves so green,
While bees wear hats, a sight unseen.
They buzz and twirl, a wild parade,
As daisies giggle in the glade.

The sun peeks in, just like a tease,
And ants are having fancy cheese!
Yet grasshoppers sing, off-key, so loud,
Pretending they're the stars, so proud.

Morning turns bright, with laughter near,
Where squirrels snack and drink a beer!
So join the fun, don't be a bore,
In the garden, life's never a chore.

A Symphony on the Garden Path

A snail composed a waltz in style,
With caterpillars dancing a mile.
A cricket played a tune off-key,
While daisies giggled, 'Let it be!'

The sunflowers swayed to music bright,
But bees were stuck in quite a plight.
Their tiny hands were all in a whirl,
As they spun circles like a girl.

A butterfly dropped a note right down,
Scribbled in hues of yellow and brown.
It said, 'Come join our wild affair,
Where we can laugh without a care!'

So gather round with flowers bold,
In harmony, let stories be told.
For laughter blooms where joy has sway,
On paths where mischief loves to play.

Beneath the Canopy of Dreams

Beneath the trees where shadows twist,
A dancing squirrel has a list,
Of acorns stashed with glee and pride,
But lost the map—it rolled and died!

The raccoons plot to steal a snack,
While rabbits hop, not looking back.
They chase their tails in silly haste,
And tumble down—oh what a waste!

The moonlight bathes the scene in glow,
As critters gather, high and low.
A frog croaks loud, a grand debut,
While wise old owl hoots, 'Who are you?'

They share their dreams of leaps and bounds,
Of music, laughter, silly sounds.
So join the fun, beneath the trees,
In this wild world, do what you please!

The Colors of Lost Time

Once flowers bloomed in colors bright,
But bees spilled paint in a wild fight.
The violets turned to shades of blue,
While poppies claimed they made a stew!

The lilies chuckled, 'Oh dear me!'
'Who knew colors could make such glee?'
As butterflies mixed up hues galore,
They painted petals—what a chore!

A hedgehog tripped on splattered hue,
Thinking it was a gooey brew.
He laughed it off, covered in stripes,
Saying, 'I'm fancy, with all these gripes!'

So paint your days in vibrant cheer,
Forget the clock; we know no fear.
For colors swirl where laughter's found,
In nature's arms, we all are crowned.

www.ingramcontent.com/pod-product-compliance
Lightning Source LLC
Chambersburg PA
CBHW071827160426
43209CB00003B/229